Nostoc

Daragh Breen

Nostoc

Shearsman Books

First published in the United Kingdom in 2020 by
Shearsman Books
1 Hicks Close
SHRIVENHAM
Oxfordshire
SN6 8FL

Shearsman Books Ltd Registered Office
30–31 St. James Place, Mangotsfield, Bristol BS16 9JB
(this address not for correspondence)

www.shearsman.com

ISBN 978-1-84861-691-2

Some of the poems in this book have previously appeared in the following journals:

'Victorian', *Shearsman* magazine; 'Nostoc', *Tears in the Fence*;
'Nostrum Nox', *Coast to Coast to Coast*; "on reading that Paula
Rego suffered…", *Blackbox Manifold*; 'Two Readings of Cy
Twombly's "Leaving Paphos…"', *Tears in the Fence*; 'Bird Movement
Above the Viaduct, N71', *Smithereens Magazine*; 'Heron & Witch'
intro-piece, *Coast to Coast to Coast*; 'A Supermoon Gives Birth to
Herself', *The Tangerine*; 'Syzygy', *Shearsman* magazine; 'Tarot',
Shearsman magazine; 'Crow with Rabbit', *Smithereens Magazine*;
'A Pair of Pig Tales' (part I only), *The Penny Dreadful*; 'Charlotte &
Emily Brontë's Irish Accents', *Banshee Magazine*; 'Do Not Despair/Do
Not Presume', *Blackbox Manifold*; 'A Pair of Shell Cases', *Southword*;
'The Bearing of the Dead Across on the Dursey…', *Blackbox Manifold*;
'A Boat-Shape of Birds' sequence, *The Fortnightly Review*.

Contents

Nostoc: a mysterious jelly-like fungus that comes to the surface after periods of rain, and which has a host of common folk names, including *witch's butter, star jelly, angel's poultice, wind-salmon spawn, pig rosettes, mist roses, Jesus's blood, beggars' pâté, paupers' stew, and goblin hearts.*

For Anne and Gerry

Hymnal for Dogs

A pack of wolves swam the shortened Irish Sea between Scotland and Ireland, resting on drifting ice, following the scent of giant Irish deer that hung like autumn over the water, their howls like bells strung over a few miles of echoing waves.

Their wolf pups would later be stolen from them, and reared and crossbred with dogs to create the alpha Irish Wolfhound, a human-mapped aberration dreamt for the purpose of hunting their own wolf ancestors.

What followed was the echo to their destruction, clouding to feed on the red robes that they'd removed, garments which they in turn left fully emptied.

Magpies, hooded crows, ravens, doctored crows, crudely engineered crows, painted crows and Scriptures' crows... all crowding across a bridge of themselves.

So much so that by 2017 A.D., it had been widely accepted that Hibernia was the Corvid Capital of the Avian Empire.

I. 1879, Kennel Club Annual Show, Dublin

It was Cromwell himself that had
set fire to the need in the dreams
of Captain George Augustus Graham
for the transmogrified original mongrel of
wolfe dogges, wolfdogs, wolfhounds;
and so he went about advertising for their
blood to re-gain possession of
what he believed to be his own soul,
using Oscar Wilde's father's surgical hands
to re-cast the breed, culling those
not self-culled by their own blue rot
of death and disease, and so his became the sole
entry in the fumbled together category
"nearest approach to the Old Irish Wolfhound".

Yet he ultimately found himself utterly
dismayed when, riverside, he stood
in the early morning January mist,
his newly fashioned dogs silent
and unwilling to hunt, and watched
transfixed as a duck scratched the
surface beneath its yellowed webbed
feet, like a Christ suddenly begin to
doubt his own ability to walk on water.

II. Victorian

i

Out in his cobbled backyard
the Reverend Jack Russell watches
a goldfinch prepare for its own funeral,
muted by the stacks of ghost-white
dog hair that it snatches from the ground.

He has been breeding for a few seasons now,
miniaturising at every step, unpacking
the Russian Doll of a fox-hunting dog
from each of the discarded ghosts.
Every dawn and dusk he has watched
the local foxes steal their red cloven way
across the fields, the tinderbox
of their nerves scurrying for sanctuary
now that the covenant has been betrayed.

ii

A fox slid out of the ivy hedging up ahead
and stalled to stare at our two dogs, their
leads harnessing them to a different world
as a brief flame of sensation shimmered
between all three, a flicker of startled memory.

Napkins of cloud were dragged through the
pewter ring of the moon, napkin tied to
napkin of night being hurried through, as a
mutiny of crows harassed each other through
a child's broken drum and the cot lurched like
a ship in hardening ice
                              – the nursery had been
disturbed, and all three had fled their disrupted
Eden.

iii

One of the dogs came back out of the ditch
head tilted upwards and proudly panting,
his mouth stuffed with the ball of a staring
rabbit's head, its ears smoothly stiff,
a medieval shuttlecock,
perfectly and neatly severed,
the veins neatly trimmed,
as if the fox had just unscrewed and
discarded it like a doll's head

of the kind that the same fox had dismantled
the winter previous, stealing about
the frozen fields in its clothes,
the frilled hems being distracted and
harassed by every thorned hedgerow.

III. Fox Donned the God-Head

Fox, wearing a God-Head mask,
stood beside the boy
and showed him;

Spring-revealed,
the Earth inheriting the meek
as angels, in their thousands,
        freefall
before re-emerging
                from the waves
with snatches of struggling silver.

Summer-revealed,
the fossil-wingspan
of the Milky Way,
the dark's original mechanism
of movement
        exposed
now flaking and crumbling.

Autumn-revealed,
all along the shore, thousands of
gulls watching
the ocean blooming
        and then withering,
blooming and then withering
with every exhausted breath.

Winter-revealed,
the dragon-life of some trees
the silent wingspan
of their roots
        dormant

beneath the quiet fields,
but always in a state of waiting.

So, where to now?
asked the boy.

Note

It should be noted that there have been some problems associated with the donning of the God-Head. When Armstrong returned from the moon, he refused to remove the old deep-sea diving helmet that he'd travelled back through the Earth's atmosphere encased in, suffering a kind of Lunar-Bends of the emotions, an ocean-weight of depression pulling on his every movement ever after.

IV. Nostoc

The female dog has spent the early part of winter
outdoors, licking and chewing witch's butter

the residue of nights of rain
and mis-formed thoughts

a regurgitated language
that she refuses to share

dressed as she is in an old gabardine school coat
and hair that she will no longer address

her womb must be squirming with
a hatchery of mermaid's purses.

It won't be long now before
she begins to dribble miniature

dogfish, skate and sharks
all which will bask briefly in the cold light of day.

Buckling about in a wind as muscular as a Clydesdale
she has wobbled away from countless strokes

yet, no matter how we try to dress her up
she continues to spill a variety of life forms.

V. Nostrum Nox

Where are you going with that blood
on your shirt, boy? the fox asked me.

I didn't recognise him at first
being out of that raggedy dress

he normally wore. He said that he'd
been out helping with the lambing

reddling the frost around the new-borns.
I told him that there was the womb

of a horse lying in our driveway,
the Trojan-night having abandoned it

there so as to transfer something else.
I asked him if he had anything to help

with the loss of an old dog. Maybe the
night will bring her back, boy, the fox said.

VI. Fox Asleep in the Middle of the Road

Wake up Fox, the boy said, please, wake up.
You're in the middle of the road.
He'd found him just lying there, with his
dress all opened-up like a hospital gown.

During the Gingerbread night
he must have tried to ford
the rivering lights, clamouring
against its unforgiving, moving sides,

a parade of Glimmer Men
making its way back to the city
having collectively dimmed the gaslight
within the smudged glass of the moon.

The gaslamp of the moon
hangs in the weak dawn.
The flock of Corvids encased
within it to detect leaks
come to the surface of its globe in a blur,
quenching its brightness.

Night lurched like an ice floe
and echoed
its own hurt like an animal
as it tried
to prise the mask of bark from its face
leaving everything exposed to
a soft dawn,
and then a sudden thunder
as a herd of reindeer all shifted direction
as one
before silence regained its hold
once more
and settled
over all that world that is
North.

"on reading that Paula Rego
suffered horrifically from depression"

I was surprised at how saddened I felt
on reading that Paula Rego suffered horrifically
from depression,
literally crawling away from her own self
on that couch,
and thought about how
the mirror of her own hauntings
had been hung with black Victorian fabric,
and the too-loud fabric of her own winding-sheet
so frightening
like the crinkling of night's dowager hump,
its deformed egg of pre-light
fabricated in the tin pot
of a Billy-in-the-Bowl.

The same tin pot that so many
of her women, condemned to bleed
and endlessly breed, squatted over
with their melon swollen thighs,
so many spilled rabbit parts
slinking into the hickory dickory
dock, as all the mice scurried
up around her neck,
which at the end of the interview
she began to squeeze and squeak,
her child's face suddenly revealed again
above a necklace of mice
that her granddaughter
had made for her.

Two Readings of Cy Twombly's
"Leaving Paphos ringed with waves"

leaving Blasket and Aran, waves heaped on all sides
the dead stain the sea with their shoals
a wound of boats begins to bleed
our rage has been winged by grief
a blood of orange dripping through the sea
ringed with wings we rage with grief

And then we went down to the currachs
                    and watched the
hordes of ghosted women in black shawls
follow the men off the train from Cork
as they trampled through the Youghal
sunshine into Clancy's pub and then peered
through a window as homemade dresses
twirled over the sliding water lilies
of light on the almost empty dance floor
of the Strand Palace next door,
                              and
then later on to the Moby Dick pub to chase
the echo of gaudy Swingboats of giddy orange
raised against a darkening sky as a shoal
of seagulls twisted and turned overhead,
gilded silver in the sieved light,
          and then to be released into the
damp July night as the music of the Funfairs
bled orange in the blue rain all the way from
Perks in Youghal to Pipers in Crosshaven, the
echo slowly blinking out from Dingle Pier to
Lahinch, from Salthill to Westport, hives of light
strung out all along the coast, with the
only music now to be found along the empty
shoreline being the low sad sound of the Merries
heard at a distance of ghost years.

leaving Inishbofin and Achill, waves mired on all sides
the dead sea stained with their shoals
we carry our grief to the waves to be washed
we stumble in waves with the weight of our dead
we are winged with waves as we bleed rage
grief-washed, we say goodbye to our dead

And then we went down to the currachs
and led them walking on their foal's oars
above the surface of the Atlantic,
lumbering forward in a swinging motion
their skeletal innards piled high
with small dull orange buoys knitted
in among the coarse once-blue netting
which we one by one began to hurl
into the sky and leave to harvest
the daily migration of seabirds

and later, when we tried to drag
the netting down, part of it had become
entangled around the tender hoof of the moon,
folded beneath the sleeping form of the beast
from which the Earth first tumbled
in a sodden mess, afraid to wake her
as she had rejected this new born at birth
and had only been fooled into a sense of
maternity when the skinned flesh of a dead
sibling was draped and pinned around it.

Rembrandt's "*The Carcass of an Ox*"

The strung-up carcass, its four limbs bound
and its belly sundered, a tapestry of inner-
workings framed and mounted for its un-
plucking, the blood having spilled from it
like a murmur of starlings fluttering
downwards through the tissue, leaving in
their wake the gull-white fatty ligaments,
an avalanche of extinguished church candles

that resembles a later self-portrait in which
the winters hang dry and scabbing on his
red jowls, their early afternoon sunsets
planed by setting frosts, the marshland stubble
from which rag-wrapped feet were pulled
like leeches, the flooded tracks that
the stray dogs patrolled, all the exposed
workings of his childhood landscape, and all
his future sorrows like a hanging threat of snow.

Cardinal, Sitting

The reds seen by the owlish light of candles
extracted from the belly of a whale,
corrugated shadows in the folds of his robes,
an arras of the history of reds
the thick woven threads dyed
from vermilion to burgundy,
the blood hues of Christ
that mark His seven last words.

The folded hare's paws of his hands
are ringed with reddled pebbles that he
discovered when he dropped the pitcher
that contained them,
the shadowed columns of his chest speak
of the manifold mysteries of his faith,

and when he stands to open the shutters
to let in the real light
four and twenty swans' necks
will fall to the floor.

The Yellow Christ

In the autumn of the world
a mother, daughter and a ghostly third
have come to this field in Northern France
to sit with Him
as He begins to wilt on His Cross.

The last of His humanity
now merely a mask,
He strains to see the three white poppies
of their bonnets, as a father
or a son or a ghostly third
walks the trench of the near laneway
marking out where all
his future sons will fall.

Insects of Utopia

Every surface was covered in moths
a savagery of tiny wings
scrapping through a debris of their own,
ants trying to excavate
and carry away the dead wings
that didn't make it to the light,
bees heavy with the powdery pollen
of moths' bodies returned to dust,
the whole massed mess incubating
pockets of larvae that gravel
the layers of piled heat,
living fossils of silverfish struggling
to stay afloat on the dust's surface,
and yet-to-be-named wingless crawl-
creatures floundering in their own
half-formed uselessness.

The idea of dusk, of a darkening,
of a permission to cease,
the offer of a coma within existence,
is a notion that has yet to be hatched
down beneath the layers
where the light-sources must
surely, at some stage, begin
to stutter, begin to blink.

X-Ray of a Wasp

A residue of flight is what is left on the screen.
The hinge that connects the hanging sack
of its lower back-end is clearly visible,
tiny but solidly held in place by six screws,
indicating that this was originally a pre-
Allen key, 23rd generation, early C20th model.

Crudely updated, the miniscule solar panels
of its blind eyes are linked by heavily plaited
coils of wires to its wings. The splinters of balsa
rigged through their sheaths are shown to be
damaged in this specimen, protruding as
they are through the membrane.

The needle work of its sting, here slightly
protruding, halted by its own malfunctioning,
its wires having seemingly become crossed,
on further magnification, to the size of a death
spike, shows a childish engraving, the scrimshaw
of its maker's mark.

Bird Movement Above the Viaduct, N71

We usually come here once a week
to clear-up the wings and things of all
those that failed to fly, their ill-conceived
wings, their wing-conceived ills, their
plastic bag and Sellotape contraptions,
their chicken wire and bed sheet fallacies,
all those boys and young men that did not
want to become those men who spend
their Februarys tramping around the
fields that surround us, hunting a fox
in the sleet, their lives measured in
the years of these dog days, their savage
need for death on a Sunday afternoon.

Sometimes, on a cold winter morning,
the light grows strange, and above
the Viaduct, a flurry of seagulls
begins to snow upwards.

From Lines Misheard

"though our tears/ Thaw not the frost which binds so dear a head!"
ADONAIS; P.B. Shelley

Like Shelley's own tangled ghost washed up drowned
within a marbled form – you had fallen, your knee shattered
and winter suddenly swept in. Your tears
could not thaw the frost that attacks the reindeer's head,
or cease the hours of rain that armour the Minotaur's crown,
or ease the centuries of sorrow that have led salmon through
blinking streams to rest in their own gravel. And then winter
crept on by, leaving you on the potholed driveway, a creature
that it had left behind, an echo of its having just passed.

The Fall of a Reindeer

(323 Reindeer Killed by Lightning, Norway, August 2016)

Woken again in the dark
by the distant echo-memory
of Mister Auden's cast
of moss-grazing reindeer
heard silvering in torrents
through their inherited streams,

their hooves that will never
be rendered down into a
treacle of animal-glue
as the moon haunts across
the back of the bedroom curtains
as they escape back into the past.

The reindeer march ever on, the
first moist-chill night still evident and
beaded on their furred antlers, the
hilt of their skulls decorated with the
dents and grooves that hold the
flames of August's blood-egg moons.

Then waking in the late summer silence
to the news that 323 reindeer
had been killed by lightning in
Norway, having grouped to
shelter each other, their antenna
coaxing the electricity down.

A mess of inter-locking antlers,
323 reindeer skins shed all at once,
their shadows running with the clouds',
while beneath the scut of a moon
out on the Burren, a landscape of
exposed catacombs, Arctic plants

survive in miniature maturity
where the residual wax of living
has dried, leaving behind its folds
of hardened husks of karst rock
that contain the relics of elk,
reindeer and wolf.

After the fourth early storm of the season
a man from the Coast Guard
explained on the radio
how the sea had been found
in a state of confusion
on the blackened rocks,
a beast still turning on itself,
a bull unsure as to whether or
not it was fully sated,
the waves hanging frills
of foaming sweat around the tired
musculature of his neck
and shoulders,
the wind mocking his slump
into a slowing calm,
a meandering of fluids,
the whole sack of him tilting
and reeling, reeling and
tilting, his whole form being warped,
again, from somewhere within.

Heron & Witch

On being born, the midwife trimmed back
the fatty webbing on her grim fists and toes
so that she would not be tempted to crawl to
water, still seemingly enthralled to a liquid world

1 Goat with Her Own Self

Her physical-self seems to wake into the night
when the car lights glide over her
finding herself tethered on a ditch
awkward between some trees
as if suddenly caught out

trying to manoeuvre herself between centuries
coming from an age of sticks and stones
ballasted by her ritual gown
and readjusting to a light
that isn't bled from handheld torches.

Daylight will reveal her alone with herself
beside the woods
January's hull
an Ark unfit
to carry any pairings of creatures.

II A Heron's Possessions

"The hooded winter lured the hooded boys into the hooded river.
Crow, Hangman, Boatman, these are the shadows that had been
affixed to their hooves while they still lay in their cradles.
These are the shadows that trailed them on every one of their walks."
old Heron lullaby

Sighted in the light of Fox Equinox,
an amber stained post-storm dawn,
with the appearance of wind-blown foam
having attached itself to some random sticks
and the notion that there is
something darker
over-crowding itself within,
pushing against the hunch of its back,
presiding over an orphanage
afloat with bloated lifeless fish,
it stands at the bend in the river
where all the young boys
slipped into the water to drown
the year all the otters began to die,
their dried-out pelts littering the
cairn-piled shore like old bits of bark,
and unfolds the lengths of its wings,
a pair of Turin Shrouds in which the
shadow of every swaddled child is still
just about visible.

III A Supermoon Gives Birth to Herself

It had been decided that all women over 65
would be examined to see if they had goats'
hooves.
        Mothers and non-mothers, bent and
spent in shawls and frost, lined the laneways
surrounding the City Hall all night.
        Many wore oven gloves
to hide the hours wasted against the rim of
the spinning-wheel, others had pinned over-
sized tin crucifixes to their borrowed long coats.

Outside of the city, that afternoon we had
watched from our window, the medieval
clockwork motion of a hedgehog shuffling to war
in the long grass, the dogs staring at it
from within their enclosure.
        A little while earlier, just on the
bend of our laneway, we had come across
a dead frog on its hunched back, as if its
tiny parachute had failed, its torso the
size of a thumb, and the dogs stopping to
stare in wonder at this one-frog plague.
        And then later, the
female dog refused to come in for the night,
sitting out in the constant rolling of the
wind, alert, as if listening for snow.

IV Joan of Arc

The universal wolf that froths the stars
comes slowly across the flat fields,
its exposed glass heart of a moon
smoked like a toad's back.

They've been burning witches again,
Dorothy of the Cross, burnt,
Alice of Maher, burnt, blaming
them for the badly growing corn.

But the gods have made a pig's ear
of the summer, the orchards are all hung
with the skins of old women, dimly
mottled and tightly wattled with rot.

When everything goes up in autumn's
smoke, the last of the colour will be lured
from the land, snatching and scratching
and gasping against the glass of the moon.

V Syzygy

Between the twin black souls
of the rabbit's eyes
the moon swam
into the shadow of the Earth
and the rats spilled their guts
hanging them out to dry
as the hares slipped their skins
and paraded on the stilts
of their hind legs

and the old women of the village
emptied their chamber pots
over the yew trees,
the Witchcraft Act having been
superseded by the universe,
for when everything is aligned
nothing is right,
every single thing is in the shadow
of the shadow of the shadow.

VI Tarot

When the weathervane dealt the cards
Jack Ketch got dealt the barge,
and in its slow, coopered wake
it trailed the bird-shells of all
the spring-eggs that he'd crushed
during his hooded days.

The reddleman and the pig-bleeder
will come at dawn to redden the skies,
as the barge hatches him in last night's
mud, his white body stretched like a
badger's back, forever scorched by that
falling star that fell across its ancestor's spine.

VII Bat & Ball

Someone had been snaring her starlings
every evening at dusk,
hiding in amongst the Leylandii,
turning them hideously inside out
before releasing them to dart around
blinded in the nearly-dark.

When she opened the stove it just lay there,
it could have been sleeping,
a thumb of smooth black fur
with little hooks for talons, and
the tiny hammocks of its dried flesh wings
unfettered and unfolded by its sides.

Holding it intently with the fire tongs,
she tried to coax its innards out with a tweezers,
first the tongue of its un-fanning tail, then the
moist ball of its downy wings, until eventually,
with the flickering of a marsupial memory, it
flung itself up towards a gathering murmur.

VIII Frogspawn

She kept it in an old metal bucket,
rusting in places,
and sitting above it on a stool,
now decades blinded,
she would scoop up fistfuls
and daub and mould it around
her deep eye-sockets,
instantly giving herself hundreds
of squirming lines of vision,
past, present and future,
so many little black pinpricks of life
reading the world for her.

30 seconds ago she saw a cat
coughing-up a dead starling
at her feet in 3 days time,
tomorrow she saw
the same starling snagging itself
in her hair last week,
enduring days of ensnared starving
in its tangled pile of curls.

She sees the rain of 5 minutes time
that will drum the worms from
the coffin of the soil
to peek at the living
that they will devour
once night finally falters and falls.

When she grows tired
of all this too-much world,
she rolls and balls the mottled-jelly
from her skull
and returns its wriggling innards

of memories to the silent
Babel of the bucket
clamped tightly between her feet.

IX Leonora Carrington's Death
Goes A-Fishing in a Heron's Mask

Mildewed in damp Altar Boy frills
a heron blows glass and drops
gobbets of liquid goblets
in to the weir's white flames.

He has swallowed too many
fish-tales down through the centuries
to be tempted now by those
of a herringbone-tweeded heathen.

Wrapped in the sleep of weeds
she silhouettes on a distant bank
and watches glass coffins of river
slide-by in the fabled evening light.

X Hedgehog on the Morning After Solstice

She slid out of the long grass
and on to the mottled tarmac
her thumb-like legs trying to steady
and balance
the unseemly weight of her fear,
her own funeral pyre
delicately carried
on the caravan of her back,
her movements slow like a tear.

A witch cast from the village
banished
blamed for the plague of incessant daylight
that had poisoned the well of the moon,
and having huddled alongside
the great wall of the house
she entered the distant wild grass
looking for relief from her burden,
to unpack the framework of her hide.

When the Red Sea was parted
the curtains of water were pinned back
so as the tea-leafing of the loaves
and the fishes could be read,
but all those things that you read
in the water,
it ain't necessarily so.

A Raven is Crowned in the West

Scratching through the wafer of its own egg,
spilling its wine about the mottled chalice
of the nest
                    – a raised curve of bone-dried
Connemara twigs, bailing twine, the husked
thorns of rusted barbed wire, fishing line,
sheep hip-bones and the matted wafts of
their snagged fleeces –
                                and having unfragmented
its egg-self, it finds itself made flesh in a sphere
of gathered fragments, and a new kingdom
that is the wild-glare of empty bogland
every where.

Crow with Rabbit

At the side of the road
the crow has undone the corset
of the rabbit's fur,
the river of its movements
having been stalled, made stagnant,
the small meat of the heart removed
its pond-life pilfered,
as the crow shuffles away in his armour.

On the seashore
Mr. Punch hunts for the purse
of Judy's heart as she lies sleeping
on the shelf of the booth.
The cold ocean is hushed to a
drowned calm as he makes away
with her stolen dowry, hunched in
his out-of-season loneliness.

A Pair of Pig Tales

i Pig Discovers Stilts

They didn't know quite what it was
when it first came into view
as they leaned on the railings
over one of the city's twin-arms of river,
something that was moving
infinitesimally slowly
through the seagulls rusty bicycle screeched fog,
it appeared to be
the carved prow of a longboat
juddering back into existence.

And then, as a pockmark cleared in the fog,
they began to discern what exactly it was,
above the low tide, above the heaped
mud-squelched banks,
four oar-like skinny legs,
and above these,
the sweating grimace of Pig's fiercely
determined face as he lifted his new legs
one by one by one by one, out of the
suck of the brown water, faltering towards
the harbour, staggering towards the cruel
hardship of the Lord-less sea.

ii Pig in Armour

It didn't suit him, to be quite honest with you,
but he had fashioned it out of old dog and food tins
bashed into shape with his own hard snout,
threaded together with twine
by his own awkward trotters.
He clanked and shimmered as he walked
around the dry yard in the hot sun,
the bulky armour moving like external rigid muscle,
believing that he was a knight
heeding a distant echo of chivalry.

He had seen a postcard of Dürer's rhinoceros
Blu-Tacked to the farmer's fridge
when he'd pass to sleep by the warmth of the stove,
and he'd heard his calling on one of those long nights,
destined to die in the frilled arms of the ferns,
his Warlord having given him up for lost,
his armour rusting throughout the winter,
the snow thawing on his shrinking body,
and come spring his tin suit
would become a shining, towering citadel
for a river of worms.

Charlotte & Emily Brontë's Irish Accents

A turf-cleaved ditch in County Down
falls from their tongues
and an arm of pewtered water is revealed,
an elongated ingot of flesh
squirming under a winter sun that sits
barely a few feet above
the horizon,
    and when it is
held aloft again
it will be above a Lancashire moor,
a host placed on an immigrant tongue,
and tasting of peat, starvation
and silence.

When Cork was still lit
in black & white,
you and your sister
once walked home in tears
from the clouds and wind of
Wuthering Heights,
    and shared a nightmare
when some dead cat fell
at both of your feet
as you passed the street's only hotel,
both of you screaming
and every window sealed shut
against the rain.

Japanese Ghost Story

For the killing of a crow
he has been encased in paper
that has been treated with cherry blossoms
and moves with
the slow faltering stutter
of the last of a winter's falling snow

his crime is inked across his surface
the crow's blood rendered as pink
as the peeled scab of spring,
he ambles through the lanes at night
and will fold himself over you
in your sleep

releasing paper birds in your dreams
that colonise
the untended cherry blossom orchard
where your much older self sits
endlessly waiting
to be beckoned forth

to the tea ceremony
at which you will remain
seated
as your much older self
struggles upright
to free themselves of your dreams.

A Pair of Shell Cases

i Snail as Prophet

After the rains
he lets himself down
out of the skull of himself,
the whole long length of wound
of himself
peeled out of the scab
of his thoughts of himself
and begins to drag
the excessive strain of himself
along the salt of the Earth.

ii Snail 'Ex Luna'

Curled-up within the solid sphere
of his world,
the hurled skull
and womb of himself,
the soon to be released
featherless form of himself

a Sputnik re-entering the Earth's orbit,
the seagull drops the shell
from a height above the promenade
to crack its casing
and drag its slimy meat
from the wreckage.

The Christ Enters Jerusalem on an Ass

Twinned within the birthing-sac
of the ass's loose skin,
we stumbled about in a
ring-a-ring-a-rosey motion,
as He steadied Himself with a
palm branch above our rumpus,
His thin heels digging into my
stomach as I tried to take
most of the weight.

Since man's recent insistence
to understand everything
only in terms of man
there was no longer any place for the
old gods to hide,
everything having been
rendered unto man,
and the land was full of scrubby
lone olive and cypress trees
where they old gods
sat amongst the sparse branches
wrapped in the slack cloths
of what were their wings.

I chose the man option, and after a
short gestation period, I found
myself with my arms wrapped
around the waist of another,
shuffling about in heavily clogged
hooves, in a world turned upside
down, where man had decided
that the gods themselves should
shoulder the weight of man.

Lobster

Were you the Christ, or was it me?
John asked of the man named Jesus

Hunkered within the armoury
of the machinations of its own
crucifixion,
it constantly contemplates
the bone-plating of its staggering
crucifix
which it regularly sheds
by hauling, hauling, hauling
itself free of it,
having forcefully burst
the membrane
that glued it to its own contrition,
leaving it momentarily mere flesh,
before once more
dragging forth about itself
the bone work
that keeps it framed
as it shuffles and crawls,
subserviently,
beneath the vast weight
of its own looming Cross.

Do Not Despair / Do Not Presume

"Do not despair, one of the thieves was an astronaut."

When Armstrong secreted some fragments
of the one true Cross in the pristine soil of
the moon, little did he know that 33 years
later, 3 enormous Crosses would have risen
to stand like ships' masts on its curve, and
as if fly-fishing, ever so slowly, cast the
line of their shadow, day-in and day-out, as
light navigates about them in a tidal dry flood.

"Do not presume, one of the thieves was a heron."

When they unpinned the large cloths of its wings
the halo of its own neck continued to hold it
aloft on its miniature Cross, the ruffle of pride
for which it had been condemned when Milton
shuffled his cards and let them all fall, a wealth
of wings and shadows like a dark snow, their
back-draught raising a chill that extinguished the
candle and hunched him further within his scarves.

The Bearing of the Dead Across
on the Dursey Island Cablecar

O'Sullivan Beare, Captain of His Nation, Chief Irish of Ireland, Lord of Bere, of Horse Island, Hog Island, Fort of the Pigs, Pig Moor, of the herds of herring ploughing through those waters as the ocean's temperature rose, their tide dragging with them the spires of Spanish fishing fleets.

A Lordship defined by the ghost-wards that the fish inhabited, bordering the rock that was frozen beneath the moss, beneath the peat, and the rivers that leaked silver and copper through his land. Ghost-wards dense with cod, haddock, salmon and mackerel all through summer. Herring and pilchard in autumn. Monkfish and plaice all year round. Beds of oysters. Nets spilling cacophonies of lobster, crabs, muscles and cockles.

Ó Súilleabháin, Osulevan, Osoleuan, O'Sullyvan, O'Swylyvan, O'Sulevan, Sullivans, Swylavan, Swylyvanm, sylvan in that remote and barbarous country that the Crown wanted for its coastal trade, burning the corn of Bantry and Beara. Called to the Tower of London in 1589, and 1592, and again in 1593 to resolve dispute after dispute, as they continued to survey the region for clearance.

~

And in the mist-muttering distance, the incomprehensible dry hark of calling to hunt the West Carbery Foxhounds from across the snow-smothered Estate of Somerville, where a congress of foxes hides beneath the pews of a church as the last shards of winter-light, that Harry Clarke has made literate, spells out their moods across the stone-flagged floor.

"…and Violet has taken to dressing like the gardener in an old trench coat, her hair wild and unkempt and frizzing in the constant drizzle. She had dismantled the hoarse car-horn from the Daimler, I found it secreted in her coat's bottomless pockets, those tattered pockets that leak constellations that give a mid-day sheen to the whole white, bright, pelt of the snow…"

~

January comes wearing wolf masks, the trees are garbed in armour and bleed fruits of crow, the shattered sleet breaks through the air and is trampled beneath into frost, the exhausting mush and slush of dragging wrapped ankles and shins that freeze in those rags of frost-flaked shivering silver. They killed twelve of their own horses, making currachs from their hides, packing their prepared flesh for meat.

North through O'Kelly Country, sleet mapped the already dead all the way back to Glengarriff; the snow so deep, as heavy as dead horses, its weight everywhere, dragging on everything. Sleet so vivid and cold, like the exposed workings of night. The cold shoals of stars crowding the night. Their fires shattering the blackness of the forests. The snow falling to the rhythm of slow bells, the moon's light echoing on its surface where it lies.

~

"…poor Violet has caught a severe chill, she just can't seem to warm up. I found her on the grounds, chasing shadows across the snow in her night-things. She says that she saw a procession of about a thousand bedraggled souls marching beneath the moon, she wanted to help them. She can only stomach porridge, and even that she has a problem trying to keep down. She just can't seem to get warm…"

As the Daimler that Edith can no longer afford to pay petrol for sits delicate as a moth beneath frost on the snow outside Somerville House, inside, the gramophone plays a sad gin-soaked New Year's Eve song for poor Violet, and all the lights in the House have been switched off in a final bid to economise.

~

With a Spanish Church bell ringing of white pointed hoods and meshed veils of black roses, his death echoed as he was stabbed, and the winter of 1601/2 once more flowed from his side, along with the trampled footprints of the 965 who had carried his blood and the glass altar of his Title through the Irish frost and snow and the medieval dying light.

And poor Edith, out on the lawn, lost in the Centuries-old fog, still looking for Violet, and Violet exiled on the moon, unloading the ships, their hulls full of snow and ice.

In January's green ocean
the slow churn of the dying day
and in the green eye of a lifting wave
a life-sized driftwood crucifix is hoisted,
the body of water bearing the great weight
upwards towards the weak light,

and just for a moment
it is suspended there
in the eerie green light,
and then the wave blinks
and the water closes,
and the Christ is drowned once more.

A Boat-Shape of Birds

"an Augur and his boy stand in the growing dark"

as he tries to teach him
how to read
the hands of the gods
prospecting
among the bird movements
sieving for nuggets

Every evening the pigeon man
at the top of the Southern Road
releases his birds to flock
in ever-increasing concentric haloes
above the crossroads, the bridge
and the South Link Road.

They expand
ever slowly
for a half-hour or so,
before beginning to contract again,
as if around the plughole
of their ramshackle shedding.

"a deer's cry"

Did you hear it?   The echo
from when Armstrong pierced the moon
with his harpoon, it finally having fallen
to Earth as slow as millennia-dead starlight,
and you and the new others decided to don
deerskins as you slipped into the fog's song
your pelts turning moist, a procession of
heavy antlers among the already dead trees
wary of Death and its whistling steel

that Thursday lunchtime that I collected you
and dropped you at the hospice,
you proudly shuffling to the reception desk
to check-in in your tracksuit,
my mother staying with you,
and as I headed back to work
there was nothing significant to see
nothing metaphorical in the sky,
where were all my birds, I thought

but four days later
when your body finally
gave up its death-gasp,
you went under
and so deep within
that you could see all the whales
carrying those old rusting harpoons
around the ocean centuries after those
that had impaled them had died.

Winter wears its caul,
from a moving train
a tree standing alone in snow
as if the world has been burnt away
around it,
the train moving backwards
through Time
bearing the bodies of the thieves,
dressed only in falconry hoods,
their twinned Crosses strapped tightly
among the bicycles,
when above a darkening field
a crow hovering on stalled wind
slid forward
                    and dropped
down
          from its shelf
into an utterly different world.

"Death enters through the West-Gate"

As the seagulls reign over the city
in a rotating crown of noise,
and the crows, at a lower realm,
unfurl the banners of
their raucousness from the tops
of bins and traffic lights,
protective of their domains through
which the pigeons constantly migrate,
none of them seem to be aware
of this morning's heron, outside the
English Market, having entered the city
along one arm of the river from the west,
hunched down into its own befuddlement,
haunted by whatever had possessed it
to witch it here, on a busy street, stock-still
and revealed by late September's light
in its nicotine bedragglement, like
smoke-stained wax
torn from the lumpy rim of a wine bottle
with two thin rills that had run loose
holding it incomprehensibly upright,
someone's Death caught bewildered
and unawares, having momentarily
forgotten who it has come for.

"leaving Island Crematorium, ringed with birds"

And the mind like the frantic
thrashing tussle of a horse
swimming in water, as seen
from beneath, its legs like
molten oars in the bubbled
wax of the river, and in reach-
ing upwards for its buoyancy,
my arms become cast in tallow,
slowly stiffening ghostly arms
inching up into ghosted realms

and then coming ashore with
your story from when you
were five years old, the night
your neighbour three fields
over died, and you went to
ask your mother why he was
knocking on your upstairs
bedroom window, and your
mother, who had grown-up
in a pre-electricity countryside,
gathered you and your brother
into her bed until your father
came home from the wake.

They came to embalm
the dead tree,
caulking it with Natron
and then waiting 40 days
for the trunk to dehydrate.
Once the chalked armour was broken off
it was wrapped tightly in linen
and placed length-ways across
two carpenter's trestles,
uncarved and unadorned,
no-longer able to seep or weep.
As they mourned this white column
a crow hovering on stalled wind
slid forward
     and dropped
down
   from its shelf
into an utterly different world.

"a sudden movement of crows
over a distance of only about 20 yards"

In the next field
about a hundred of them
lifted off the ground and began
to swirl
like the twisted hem
of a skirt

the air full of the anxious sounds
of gulls above a hull of mackerel

then they passed in a low cortège
over our bungalow
and steadied as if one
to dock against the giant dark wall
of the Leylandii

and then just as suddenly
fell silent
once more
as if returning to mourn for existence.

*"what words sparked the crows
from the silence of the ground?"*

As their myriad black forms
rose from late September's field
and stalled there briefly,
just hanging,
pinned to autumn's light

      and the realisation
      that we were left bearing
      a carcass of words without meaning

as when the God-lie was detected
on observing a parasitic wasp,
meticulously crafted and designed,
inject her eggs
deep within a caterpillar
giving her off-spring an instant
feast of beast
from which to emerge
with fulsome
fluttering translucent wings.

One Easter,
having been haunted by days
of constant scratching,
we removed the steel plate
from the ash-box of our stove
and one still-living crow dragged
itself out into the light, crashing again and
again against glass until finding the door.
We removed another two,
dead and embedded in a huge crown
of twigs and branches, and
as we buried them, above us,
a crow hovering on stalled wind
slid forward
                          and dropped
down
          from its shelf
into an utterly different world.

"a boat-shape of birds rows itself across the sky"

For months after you died
I tried to describe the birds
above the city as I stared out
from within a sheep's skull,
knowing that the light had gone
to weed and would soon ivy
with night. But all that I saw
was dust, kicked-up by the
ghosts of white dancing Spanish
horses,
       and as it fell, it was
briefly paused, as the world
itself was briefly stalled in its
fall from orbit,
          and in the
void I could hear the sound of
emptiness as melancholic as
whale-song, its vast distances
suddenly recognisable as the
dust of stars became visible
on the manes of these Celestial
horses, paused for our lifetime
in their own brief moments,
as their spirits switched direction.

"Piper's Funfair winter grounds, Douglas, an echo"

Something unseen
sparks a slump of seagulls
to spin-up off the river
with Chair-O-Plane screams
and rotate as if confined
within a Wall of Death

as beyond the light
a silt of stars
gets pushed-out
just that little bit further,
like a Coin Pusher Machine
in an Arcade

and then just as abruptly,
like the jellyfish-collapse
of a Big Top tent,
the seagulls flop and
drop to echo
out across the river's surface,

and the stars remain silted
at the edge of the universe
as dark's tide is brought
to a hushed silence,
and it has grown so quiet that
you could hear a planet drop.

Lightning Source UK Ltd.
Milton Keynes UK
UKHW011449191219
355682UK00001B/87/P